MW00929895

This book belongs to

Made in the USA
Monee, IL
31 January 2021

59170030R00069